Botticelli in the Fire received its first European
performance at Hampstead Theatre, London, on
18 October 2019. The cast, in alphabetical order, was
as follows:

Leonardo da Vinci Hiran Abeysekera
Poggio di Chiusi Stefan Adegbola
Sandro Botticelli Dickie Beau
Lorenzo de Medici Adetomiwa Edun
Madre Maria Louise Gold
Clarice Orsini / Venus Sirine Saba
Girolamo Savonarola Howard Ward

Director Blanche McIntyre
Designer James Cotterill
Lighting Designer Johanna Town
Sound Designer Christopher Shutt
Composer Olly Fox
Movement Director Polly Bennett
Casting Director Juliet Horsley CDG

Botticelli in the Fire

Jordan Tannahill is a playwright, author, and director. His plays have been translated into ten languages and widely honoured in Canada and abroad. He received the Governor General's Literary Award for Drama in 2018 for *Botticelli in the Fire* and *Sunday in Sodom,* and in 2014 for *Age of Minority: Three Solo Plays.* His other plays include *rihannaboi95* (Dora Award for Outstanding New Play), *Concord Floral* (Dora Award for Outstanding New Play), *Late Company* (West End, 2017), *Sunday in Sodom* (Toronto Theatre Critics' Award for Best New Play), and *Declarations* (Canadian Stage, 2018). His virtual reality performance *Draw Me Close* (National Theatre, UK/National Film Board of Canada), premiered at the 2017 Tribeca Film Festival and is currently touring internationally. Most recently, he wrote the text for two of choreographer Akram Khan's pieces, the Olivier Award-winning *Xenos* (2018), and *Outwitting the Devil* (2019). He is the author of *Theatre of the Unimpressed: In Search of Vital Drama* (2015), and the novel *Liminal* (2018).

also by Jordan Tannahill from Faber

LATE COMPANY

JORDAN TANNAHILL

Botticelli in the Fire

ff

FABER & FABER

First published in an edition with *Sunday in Sodom*
by Playwrights Canada Press, Toronto, 2018

This edition first published in 2019
by Faber and Faber Ltd
74–77 Great Russell Street
London WC1B 3DA

Typeset by Country Setting, Kingsdown, Kent CT14 8ES
Printed in England by CPI Group (UK) Ltd, Croydon CR0 4YY

A CIP record for this book is available from the British Library

978-0-571-36016-1

2 4 6 8 10 9 7 5 3 1

Botticelli in the Fire premiered at Canadian Stage's Berkeley Street Theatre, Toronto, in repertory with *Sunday in Sodom*, on 26 April 2016. The cast was as follows:

Sandro Botticelli Salvatore Antonio
Clarice Orsini Nicola Correia-Damude
Lorenzo de Medici Christopher Morris
Girolamo Savonarola Alon Nashman
Madre Maria Valerie Buhagiar
Leonardo da Vinci Stephen Jackman-Torkoff

Director Matjash Mrozewski
Set and Costume Designer James Lavoie
Lighting Designer Steve Lucas
Composer and Sound Designer Samuel Sholdice
Projection Consultant Cameron Davis
Fight Director Simon Fon

Characters

Sandro Botticelli
an art star in his thirties

Clarice Orsini
a rich and powerful woman in her mid-thirties

Lorenzo de Medici
a rich and powerful man in his early forties

Leonardo da Vinci
a painter in his early twenties

Poggio di Chiusi
a painter and bon-vivant in his thirties

Madre Maria
a woman in her fifties

Girolamo Savonarola
a charismatic friar in his sixties

BOTTICELLI IN THE FIRE

Act One

Spotlight on Sandro Botticelli entering the audience from stage door. He holds an open bottle of wine in his free hand.

Sandro Do you know what –
    Sorry just before we start the show
    Do you know what they just asked me in the greenroom?
    If I'd stick around after the show to sign calendars
        in the lobby
    A calendar of my paintings
    Uh – no fucking way
    Sorry
    Proceeds go to some sick actors fund or something
    Uh sorry *no*

Takes a swig of wine.

Oh, and turn off your fucking cell phones
Alright?
Go on
Take them out
This is real, I'll wait
This has been five hundred years in the making
If I hear a ding I'll kill you
I'm serious

I was talking with a friend the other day and he said:
'Don't you think performing a play about yourself is
    a bit of a vanity project?'
And I was like: one, this is not just a play it's an
    extravaganza
and two, vanity?

If you had an eternity to tell yourself the same story
      over and over
to pick apart every mistake
eventually you'd want an audience too
Because where do you go from here?
Where does it end?
Another five hundred years, over and over – no
No
It stops tonight
Vanity project
Fuck you very much

And I promise you this isn't going to be another
      tortured fag-artist sob story
Okay maybe it is – sue me
But seriously, it's more of a downfall story
And we all like a good downfall, don't we?
Especially when you're the King Shit
And I was, for a time

State dinners
Commissions
They called me a wunderkind
They called me the poster child of my generation
I painted the fucking Sistine Chapel
Not the ceiling, mind you
just the floor-level frescoes – but still

*In pools of light appear Clarice Orsini, Lorenzo
de Medici, Savonarola, Poggio di Chiusi, and Madre
Maria, singing a choral overture, which continues
under the following text.*

Clarice The thing you gotta know about Botticelli is
      he had a huge . . . talent
Definitely the biggest I'd ever seen
And he knew how to use it
Other men – they always know when a guy's got
      a huge talent

4

Just the way he carried himself
It made them mad with envy
Botticelli had that swagger
He'd be walking down the street and you'd think
    to yourself
'Goddamn what a great fucking painter he must be'

Sandro I was at the Medici's palace three times a week

Lorenzo If Botticelli wasn't at a party, no one would stay –

Sandro I was their confidant

Lorenzo – and somehow he managed to be at four
    or five in one night

Clarice He had such a big talent, men and women
    fainted as he walked past

Poggio Oh let's be honest he was the most voracious
    bottom in Florence

Savonarola A man of a thousand lovers they said

Maria Even as a baby he was insatiable

Sandro Ma

Maria Well it's true

Clarice He had such a big talent, dogs barked at it
    and then ran away whimpering

Maria As a baby I would catch him fondling himself
    in his crib

Sandro Momma please / I'd rather you –

Maria I didn't know what to do
    I asked my husband and he just laughed and shrugged
    I asked my mother and she told me to say fifty –

Chorus – Hail Mary full of grace!

Sandro When she asked our priest –

Maria Father, what do I do with Sandro he won't stop
        touching himself
    He said 'Bring him back in seven years and I'll take
        care of it myself'

Chorus laugh.

    I'm joking
    The priest said:

Sandro 'Tie his hands to the bars of the crib'

Maria So that's what I did
    I tied his hands to the bars

Poggio Well that explains a few of your predilections

Sandro The point I was trying to make was –

Savonarola The tabloids loved him of course

Sandro There was a time / when I was –

Savonarola He was absolutely

Sandro   – ubiquitous

Poggio Girl was fierce

Savonarola And his depravity –

Sandro People would come up to me at a party
    and they'd be just dripping with jealousy
    I remember this one queen, he said to me
    'I heard you once had an orgy with thirty people that
        lasted a whole weekend'
    And I was like: 'Once?'
    Please
    Do your research girl
    Do. Your. Research.
    Once
    Cute

Poggio The truth is –

Sandro I was a dog
  A dog doesn't understand moderation
  A dog eats till it pukes
  And when I was living I was *living*
  I was eating the marrow from the fucking bone

Poggio But in those days –

Sandro Everyone was dying young and beautiful
  and I thought well fuck if that's the case then –

Poggio No limits girl

Sandro I wanted to live so badly it was like a madness
  'Cause I knew there wasn't anything after

  Gestures around.

  Just the fucking void
  I was so fucking terrified of the void
  But y'all are, don't think I don't know
  Everyone was back then too
  Scared shitless
  They prayed and prayed and prayed – bless
  Me?
  I was going to wring every last drop outta life while
    I could

  Lights shift.
    Leonardo appears beside Sandro, standing in his
  Renaissance finery.

Leonardo You look like you crawled out of a back alley

Sandro Leo

Leonardo This is your gala Sandro
  People've travelled from across the / country to
    celebrate you –

Sandro I know I know, I –

Leonardo – can't show up to the Medici's palace looking like you've been doing lines of coke off a toilet seat

Sandro I'm sorry

Leonardo Here

Leonardo begins to undress.

Sandro What're you doing?

Leonardo Put this on

Leonardo hands Sandro his tunic and jacket. Sandro hands him his soiled shirt.

Sandro Oh, and did you remember –?

Leonardo Yes yes

He hands Sandro a stylised carnival plague-doctor's mask.

Sandro Ugh why do I have to be the plague doctor?

Leonardo Because you're one with the big nose

Sandro It just feels in bad taste

Leonardo Exactly, it's perfect for you

Sandro takes Leonardo's face in his hands and looks into his eyes.

Sandro You're lucky you're so cute

Poggio appears beside them wearing a half-mask and holding two glasses of champagne.

Poggio Well about fucking time
I was starting to think you were going to blow off your own party

Poggio hands him one of the champagne flutes.

Sandro Oh my God bless you

He downs the drink as Poggio lifts his mask to size Leonardo up.

Poggio And speaking of blowing off this must be the new apprentice

Sandro Leo, this is Poggio di Chiusi

Poggio I've heard so much about you

Sandro (*to Leo*) We apprenticed together back in the day

Poggio I taught this fucker everything he knows

Sandro Please if you taught me everything I know you'd be arrested

Poggio Little word of advice sweetie: don't fall in love with him
All his new apprentices do and it breaks my heart

Leonardo Thanks, I'll take it under advisement

Sandro My God look at the turnout

Poggio Frankly I'm surprised anyone came at all

Sandro Well fuck you very much

Poggio Because of the protests

Sandro Ugh, I mean leave those shopfronts alone am I right?

Poggio Listen, if I wasn't here with you tonight I'd be out there too
People are poor, we're living in shit-holes, and we're getting sick

Sandro And smashing things is not helping

Poggio Well the Medici sure the hell aren't either

Sandro They have a lot on their plate

Leonardo Yeah while everyone else is starving

Poggio Sing it

Light shift. A masquerade party. Sandro turns to the audience.

Sandro (*to audience*)
There were hundreds of people in the ballroom
everyone peering in my direction but too shy to
　　approach
So the three of us were this little island in a sea
　　of fawning acolytes
until all of a sudden a hush fell over the crowd and
　　from across the room –

Lorenzo and Clarice appear in their royal regalia, wearing golden masks.

Poggio My God there they are

To Leonardo.

Lorenzo the Magnificent and his wife Clarice Orsini

Sandro Do you reckon that's real gold?

Poggio Girl there's two giraffes in the back garden
Yes, that's real gold

Lorenzo lifts his mask to address the gala.

Lorenzo Ladies and gentlemen
it's my great pleasure to welcome you all here this
　　evening

Sandro (*to Leonardo*) How do I look?

Leonardo Roguish

Lorenzo We are in the midst of a rebirth
A rebirth in the ideals of art and science that once
　　brought greatness to our ancient brothers

And in these trying times it is the arts in particular
which give us an opportunity to consider that which
    lifts us
  that which unites us
  and that which makes us human
  We are here tonight to celebrate a man who
  through his divine gift
  reflects back to us our humanity

Poggio (*murmuring to Leonardo*)
  Let's be honest we're here because of the open bar

Lorenzo A man who masterpiece by masterpiece
  is pulling us by the balls out of the Dark Ages and
    into the light
  Into a world built on the bedrock of reason and fact
  not the shifting sands of ignorance and fear
  Tonight we honour a man I am proud to also call
    a close friend

Poggio (*murmuring to Sandro*)
  He can afford to buy as many friends as he wants

Sandro And don't you wish you were one of them?

Poggio Friends come and go, babe
  enemies accumulate

Lorenzo It gives me immense pleasure tonight to bestow
    the Order of San Marco
  to none other than Sandro Botticelli

*Light shift. The gala falls away. Sandro is once more
by himself.*

Sandro The crowd erupted and parted for me like the
    Red Sea
  as a hundred white balloons fell from the ceiling
  and after Lorenzo pinned the medallion to my chest
    and shook my hand

I shook hands with Clarice
and as we did something passed between us
our eyes lingering a second too long
She found me by myself on the balcony later that night

Spot appears on Clarice's face; she is standing right beside Sandro.

Clarice If I have to make any more small talk I'm going to smash this glass and cut someone's throat

Sandro Well I
hope I don't disappoint

Clarice lights a cigarette.

Clarice When people down there see pictures of tonight all of us dressed up like this, toasting your brilliance what do you think goes through their minds?

Sandro What . . . a bunch of fucking assholes

Clarice And do you know what my husband thinks they're thinking?

Sandro shakes his head.

Wow
The Medici are pulling us by the balls out of the Dark Ages

Sandro Right

Clarice The streets are burning

Sandro People are –

Clarice – furious, of course they are, wouldn't you be? The plague is back
There are bodies rotting in the streets

Sandro (*to audience*)
   I couldn't believe she was speaking so candidly
   And then, as if catching herself –

Clarice I don't know why I'm saying this to you

Sandro What do you think should be done then?
   To stop the plague

   Beat.

Clarice Would you believe
   that's
   the first time anyone's asked me that

Lorenzo (*calling from offstage*) Clarice!

Clarice I'm sorry
   You know how possessive he can be

Sandro I want to hear your ideas

Clarice Well I'm afraid that'll have to wait for one of
   our sessions

Lorenzo (*calling from offstage*) Clarice!

Sandro Sorry one of our –?

Clarice Did Lorenzo not mention the commission?

Sandro Uh . . . no

Clarice Oh
   Well it just so happens the award comes with a
   big commission

   She finishes her cigarette and flicks it away.

   To paint me

   Blackout.

TWO

The sounds of intense orgasms fill the space.

A large canvas is on an easel in the middle of the room, below which are sprawled the naked bodies of Sandro and Clarice. Sandro's face is buried below the sheets and Clarice screams in ecstasy. He is eating her out, and doing a great job at it.

After a moment Sandro pops his head up from under the sheets to catch his breath.

Sandro Maybe we should –

Clarice I swear to God if you stop –

> *Sandro dives back under the bedsheets and Clarice moans with renewed vigour.*
> *Leonardo enters the room with a handful of mail, notices the amorous pair, and exits unseen.*
> *Clarice climaxes thunderously.*
> *Sandro pops his head back out of the sheets.*

Sandro For the record when I suggested we eat out, I meant breakfast

Clarice Was I too rough?

Sandro (*adjusting jaw*) No I'm good

> *Clarice runs her hand through Sandro's hair.*

Clarice Hey

Sandro Hey

Clarice That was nice

Sandro Mmm

> *They kiss.*

Clarice What time is it?

Sandro (*looking for his phone*) Where's my –?
Ugh . . . it's too far

Clarice Your little butt boy will be here any minute

Sandro I wish you'd stop calling him that
Especially to his face

Clarice rises.

Clarice I should wash up

Sandro We really can't do this every morning

Clarice Why?
Because of Lorenzo?
I've told you, we barely sleep in the same palace any
more

Sandro I just –

Clarice It's fine

She is now offstage.

(*Calling.*) In case you haven't noticed
there are other things on his mind

*Sandro flops back into the sheets and begins jerking
off. Leonardo enters.*

Leonardo Morrrrning

*Sandro immediately desists masturbating and acts
nonchalant.*

Sandro You're early

Leonardo The new horsehair fine-tips arrived in the mail

Sandro Fabulous

Leonardo (*looking through mail*)
Would you like to make a donation to help repatriate
the relics of St Peter back to –

Sandro No

Leonardo The rest are bills

Sandro Put them on the table, I'll deal with it

Leonardo Are you visiting your mother today?

Sandro Fuck is it already Sunday?

Leonardo Seems like your hands are a little full

Sandro That's two weeks in a row, that's so bad
I just –

He glances at the canvas and stops.

Jesus Christ

Leonardo What?
Oh I stayed late to fix the feet last night
I know they were giving you some trouble

Sandro Uh huh

Leonardo It's just a – fix

Sandro Right

Leonardo If you –

Sandro I was going to deal with them today

Leonardo I know
I just –

Sandro nods. Pause.

I can change them back if you don't –
you know

Pause.

Sandro Leo can I ask you something?

Leonardo nods.

Sandro How did you do this?

Pause.

I mean this – (*Imitating the pose of Venus's right foot.*)
How her foot feels rooted now as if it's really –
(*Gestures.*) The shading here (*Points.*)

Leonardo I don't know I just –

Sandro It's good
It's very good

Leonardo registers the compliment for a moment.

Leonardo Well if you don't mind me making another
    suggestion
Zephyr right now?
We don't get any sense that he's connected to Venus's
    movement or the waves
I mean it doesn't even look like he's blowing
For all we know he's about to you know
    (*Mimes vomiting.*) puke or something
So my suggestion, and I know this sounds a bit literal
    but few little wisps of breath
a few dashes of white / right here could really –

Sandro Right, well why don't we –

Leonardo Look

He takes up the paint pallet.

Sandro Heyheyhey

Leonardo Just –

*Leo applies a few brisk dashes of white to the canvas.
He stands back and both he and Sandro consider the
results.*

Sandro (*impressed*) Okay

Leonardo See?
  Now it's –
  It connects it, right?
  We get a sense that he's –

Sandro He's the wind

Leonardo Right
  And speaking of which do you mind if I open a
    window?

Sandro (*still processing Leonardo's intervention in the
  painting*) What?

Leonardo It's just a little musty in here

Sandro No, no, no the protests disturb Clarice

Leonardo Uh huh

Sandro We –

Leonardo Her cum is still on your face by the way

  Sandro wipes his mouth.

Sandro We were just –

Leonardo I know

Sandro She runs this city
  She could have me thrown in prison

Leonardo How romantic

  *The sound of the shower turning on. He tosses Sandro
  a book from his knapsack.*

  Oh thanks for this by the way

Sandro You're already done?

Leonardo I can see why it's inspired you

Sandro So?

Leonardo It's good

Sandro Babe, the *Metamorphoses* is more than good
Jupiter turning himself into a shower of gold to seduce
Danaë?

Leonardo (*laughing*) Yeah that was something

Sandro And then a bull and a cloud
I mean *that's* a god

Leonardo I guess

Sandro Have you never felt yourself transformed like that?

Leonardo You know, it got me thinking – Venus
How appropriate really
Goddess of beauty, yes, but also perpetually dissatisfied
Always desiring something greater for herself
Married to Vulcan, a powerful god, sure
but also a dull metal worker, totally banal
No sex, no fun, no interesting conversations
So Venus goes looking / for better company elsewhere –

Sandro Leo

Leonardo – and finds the delectable Mars and naturally
they start fucking until –

Sandro She's a means to an end

Leonardo Is everyone?

Sandro Are you being a little grumpy bitch this morning?

Leonardo There were two bodies at the end of the street
this morning covered in bedsheets
No one will touch them or go near them –

Sandro Listen –

Leonardo – and it's like you're pretending not to notice

Sandro What do you think I'm doing here?

With her? With this painting?
When the plague comes I'm going to need / friends in
    high places
With influence

Leonardo The plague is already here, it's on our doorstep

Sandro The best doctors, the best medicine
    How do you think I'm going to get that?

Leonardo Well I'm glad you've worked it all out

Sandro Sweetie: listen to me
    We are modern people
    This is the fucking Renaissance
    The earth is round
    The earth goes around the sun
    We're not going to die of the plague

Leonardo Because the Medici will –

Sandro – pull me favours, yes

Leonardo You're fucking his wife

Sandro Sometimes I wonder if they, like –

Leonardo What?

Sandro Like maybe they have some kind of arrangement

Leonardo Wait you think he *knows* that you're / fucking
    his wife

Sandro takes out his phone

Sandro Look at this text he sent me last weekend

Leonardo (*reads text*) Huh

Sandro 'How's the painting cumming along?'
    Coming spelt with a 'u'

Leonardo Could be an autocorrect

Sandro Right

Leonardo Or a typo
I mean the 'u' and the 'o' are very close on the keypad

Sandro Listen I've been around long enough to know:
the elites are all perverts
They have their little games
and if you can play by their rules they'll take care
of you
And when the shit goes down, we're going to need
their –

*Clarice walks out of the bathroom, holding a large
white towel.*

Clarice Sandro, did you steal these towels from the palace?

*She notices Leonardo and wraps herself up in the
towel, suddenly more self-conscious.*

Sandro Ha, funny you should mention that –

Clarice Do you think it's a bit much?
I suddenly had this doubt in the shower about the pose
That maybe it's all a little –

Sandro Much

Clarice Debauched

Sandro Clarice hi I'm Botticelli, debauched is what I do
If your husband wanted you in a nun's habit he should
have commissioned Fra Filippo

Clarice But is it in good taste?
I mean it's just – such a departure

Sandro From good taste?

Clarice From everything else, you know, out there

Sandro Precisely, why should I just add another canvas
to the heap of 'everything else out there'?

Clarice He doesn't know it's a nude

Sandro He must

Clarice I don't think so

Sandro Just tell him a painter can't ignore inspiration

Clarice I think he was hoping to put this in the dining
room though

Sandro Clarice enough, you're stressing me out
(*To Leonardo.*) Put on my Chill Out playlist will you?

Leonardo exits.

Clarice I prefer our sessions when we're alone

Sandro Yes, but those are terribly unproductive

Clarice Besides, I can tell he hates me

Sandro Don't be ridiculous

Clarice Was he another hustler you pulled off the street?

Sandro No no he's the bastard son of a farm girl from
Vinci

Clarice Well I don't trust him

Sandro Leonardo?
He's been with me three months

Clarice There's just something about him
Still, fabulous bone structure, don't you think?
You could cut an apple with his jaw

Sandro Honestly? He's the real fucking deal
It took him three hours to learn how to mix tempera
with egg yolk
It took me three months
A couple mornings ago I came in here and he'd fixed
your mouth

I couldn't even tell what he'd done but it was suddenly
    perfect
I sketched an angel and he corrected my proportions
The length of her arm, the distance between her
    collarbone and waist
He doesn't even realise how brilliant he is

*Sandro crosses to the easel and begins getting ready to
work.*

Clarice You have a little crush

Sandro Please

Clarice You do, look at you
I haven't seen you like this before
All earnest

Sandro No no he's just a little – puppy dog tugging
    on his leash
woof woof you know

Clarice God that makes me –

Sandro What?

Clarice The way you look at him

Sandro Come here

They kiss. Music begins to play.

Clarice Which reminds me
This morning Lorenzo was saying how much he misses
    your squash games

Sandro Did he?
How sweet

Clarice I was supposed to tell you
he wants to see you on the court tomorrow at ten a.m.

*Leonardo returns and begins mixing paint while
observing the other two.*

Sandro What?

Clarice Just bring your runners, he has rackets

Sandro glances towards Leo (and does so periodically throughout the rest of the scene.)

Sandro I have – brunch plans

Clarice Well you'll just have to cancel them
He'll send along a driver at quarter-to

Sandro You've been here for two hours and / you tell me now

Clarice I didn't want to spoil the mood

Sandro Are you fucking with me?

Clarice Excuse me?

Sandro Yes you are look at you fucking with me

Clarice No I am / not fucking with you

Sandro Do the two of you –?

Clarice What?

Sandro Does he know?

Clarice No
Why are you even –?
Have you said / something?

Sandro Of course I haven't

Clarice 'Cause I'd have your tongue cut out

Sandro Then –?

Clarice Do you have any idea how much he talks about you?
You quiet his mind Sandro

Sandro We have – a special connection

24

Clarice And he's anxious to see the canvas

Sandro Anxious?

Clarice Yes but I told him / he'd just have to wait

Sandro I just want to make sure we're all on the same
    page

Clarice There's only one page to be on

Sandro Well, thank you for the invitation
    You can tell him –

Clarice You can just tell him: you were inspired

She resumes her pose.

Oh and do me a favour
Stop looking at the boy

Light shift.

THREE

Spotlight appears on Sandro. He speaks to the audience.

Sandro
I know what you're thinking:
    shit girl
Watch yourself
Yes
Oh yes
These were dangerous times
And if you wanted to survive,
    not just survive
but maybe even thrive a little,
    if you could be so lucky
you had to play a lot of sides,
    alright

Chorus
(*faintly, in halting
soprano*) one-tenth
is a quarter

below the knee

to the root

one-tenth

you had to play so many sides	eyes
you didn't even know what game	
you were playing any more	knee

In the upstage shadows, cloaked figures in plague-doctor masks carry bodies one by one and pile them as if in a mass grave.

And Leo was right	breasts
The plague was back	
I remember years ago when I was	one-eighth
a kid	one-sixth
	is a quarter

Lights up faintly on Maria.

Maria   below the foot

My goodness my little Sandro	
had nightmares	to the root
Nightmares all the time	of a man
He'd wake up in the middle of	
the night screaming and crying	
and he'd run into my room	eyes
tears streaming down his face	
'Sweetie what's wrong?'	knee
In his dreams he told me he saw	
his skin peeling off his body	
I held him, I rocked him	breasts
Of course he had seen the images	
on TV	
The plague, the piles of bodies	
in the streets	one-tenth
'Sweetie, you don't have to worry	is a quarter
You're not going to get the plague'	is
'Why?' he'd ask	
'Because only sinners get the	
plague	eyes
And you – your soul is like a	
cloud	knee

White and incorruptible
Beyond the reach of the hands
  of men'   breasts
I remember one night, to get him
  to stop crying
I took him into the kitchen and made
  him a peanut-butter sandwich
because I knew that was his favourite
I remember I stepped out for a moment
  to use the toilet
and when I returned
I saw Sandro take the knife out of
  the peanut butter and lick it like this

Maria and Sandro demonstrate licking peanut butter off a knife.

Maria Down one side
  and then down the other
  so slowly
  savouring the taste
  eyes closed
  lost in it
  letting nothing go to waste
  He didn't know I saw him
  But I did, from the doorway of the kitchen
  It was only an instant
  But in that moment I saw
  how bottomless his pleasure was
  And it terrified me

Light shift. The plague doctors continue to drag and pile bodies in the background.

Sandro At night Poggio and I would hit the town hard
  and I mean can't-find-your-way-home-don't-remember-
    your-name-hard
  And one morning, a couple months before the gala

the sun was coming up, people were just beginning
    to open their shops
when all of a sudden across the street –

*Lights raise faintly on Savonarola. He is speaking into
a microphone and a portable amp.*

Savonarola Fleas
    Let me tell you about fleas
    Fleas feast on the blood of others
    Fleas feast on the blood, sweat and tears of others
    sucking money from the Church and the people
    to fill their homes with gold and jewels and blasphemous
        art as the people starve

Sandro This like ridiculous street preacher foaming at
    the mouth

Savonarola These fleas we call the Medici
    and the artists and opportunists who get fat off
        the Medici
    Let me tell you about fleas
    Fleas spread the plague

Poggio What does he think this is, some small town in
    the south?

Savonarola The city is sick with the pestilence of sin
    And like Sodom and Gomorrah its day of reckoning
        is near

Poggio (*laughing*) Sodom and –

Sandro I pitied him really

Poggio You've got to be kidding

Sandro People are educated here
    They talk to God, if at all, quietly and privately

Savonarola Brothers and sisters we have all been
    distracted!

Sandro This was one of the most progressive cities in
    the world

Savonarola In this age of darkness we have been
    distracted from the one thing that truly matters
    and that is our soul
    That is the one thing the plague cannot touch
    And to the fleas that suck our blood
    We will pinch them off one by one
    We will burn them with matches
    We will be the hailstorm that breaks the heads of
      those / who do not take shelter

Poggio lunges and grabs Savonarola's microphone.

Poggio Honey this is the worst karaoke song I've ever
    heard in my life
    Why don't you try / 'Girls just wanna have fun,
      that's all they reeeeaaaally waaaant'

Savonarola Get your – let – get off of me

*Lights fade on Poggio as he and Savonarola wrestle
over the microphone, Poggio singing Cyndi Lauper's
'Girls Just Want to Have Fun'*

Sandro It's amazing how much can change in a few
    months

FOUR

Lights rise on the set of a television news talk show.
    *The Host (played by the same actor who plays
Lorenzo) sits in an armchair across from Savonarola. The
interview is filmed via live-feed camera and projected on
the massive wall behind them. We cut in on the interview
mid-flow.*

Host But seriously, here you are, the year's big overnight
    success story –

Savonarola You know, I, I keep hearing this and I'm –
(*Chuckles*.) Listen I'm in my late fifties
I've been working at this a long time
This doesn't just happen overnight

Host But you have to admit it's been a hell of a few
months

Savonarola Well –

Host A bestselling book, huge turnouts at your sermons –

Savonarola Right but this is not about me
This is what the press and the Medici don't seem
to understand
This is about returning power to the people from
a corrupt elite
that is profoundly out of touch with their lives
and profoundly out of touch with God

Host Sure but –

Savonarola The Medici are bankers!
(*Chuckles*.) They're just a family of usurers, they're
not kings, they're not gods
But we've let them think they are
And now they're treating the city like their personal
wallet

Host But this isn't really about corruption for you, is it?

Savonarola Well –

Host In terms of –

Savonarola Well it is about corruption, of course it is
The deepest kind of corruption
Why do you think the Lord sent this plague?

Beat.

Host Are you –?

Savonarola I'm asking you, yes

Host I –

He lifts his hands as if to say 'Who am I to answer that question?'

Savonarola The Medici are trying to put Man, put
       themselves at the centre of the universe
and we're saying no
No to their pagan gods and golden idols made by
       their sodomite artists
Sodomites who are celebrated and walking the streets
not even making an attempt to hide what they are

Host You seem to be particularly / preoccupied with –

Savonarola Have you been, sorry to interrupt, but have
       you been to the countryside lately?
I'm from the countryside
Do you know what people's nickname for Florence
       is there?

Host I can imagine

Savonarola God is unequivocal in fact there are few
       things He is so unequivocal about as sodomites
Frankly, we're lucky all He's sent us is the plague

Host What would you say to the people –
Because there were a lot of people upset with the
       Medici before you came along

Savonarola Sure

Host So what would you say to those who might say
       okay well I hate the Medici, they're corrupt, the plague
       is back, they're not doing anything
but this Savonarola guy is just too –

Savonarola Extreme

Host *Way* too extreme for me
Calling for children to spy on their parents
For sex workers to be chastised
for the streets to be policed for indecent dress
A hotline for neighbours to report on their neighbours

Savonarola Wake up
That's what I say to them
This is a war for people's souls
And you're either standing with God or you're
standing in His way

*Image cuts to static. Sounds of protests in the
darkness.*

FIVE

Lights up on Sandro's studio.
*Sandro, Poggio, and Leonardo stagger through the
door.*
*The canvas is turned away from the audience, covered
in a tarp.*

Poggio And I looked him in the eye and I said 'Sweetie
you better drop that knife
'cause I refuse to be killed by someone wearing taffeta
sleeves'

Sandro You've got to draw the line somewhere

Poggio Slashes and puffed no less

*Sandro runs his thumb along a gash on Leonardo's
forehead.*

Sandro It'll probably leave a scar

Leonardo Shit, really?

Poggio You're too pretty anyway, it's disgusting

Sandro We just gotta accept you guys can't be seen
walking around with me any more
It's too dangerous

*He grabs a cloth and some rubbing alcohol from
his work bench. Sandro sits Leonardo down and
administers the alcohol to his wound.*

Poggio Honey, we were all there screaming with our
wine spritzers
We were not exactly being discreet, 'specially not
Angelo

Sandro Plus, I probably shouldn't have flashed my dick
at them

Poggio (*laughing*) No you shouldn't have

Sandro But let's be honest that's what all those assholes
secretly want anyway

Poggio You know the fucked-up thing is I recognised
two of those guys
They were there with me at the first protests
I was there at the first fucking one handing out bottles
of water
and now they're throwing a wine spritzer in my face
I have to walk an extra five blocks home now just to
avoid the protests

Sandro The walking will do you good girl

Poggio I stood shoulder to shoulder with those people
and now he's turned them into I don't know what
Some crazed fuckin' God-mob

Leonardo What was that word they started shouting
at us?

Poggio Faggots

Leonardo What does that even mean?

Poggio Bundles of wood

Leonardo I'm sorry?

Sandro Bundles of –?

Poggio Faggots are kindling

Silence.

Sandro Lorenzo's losing his grip on the city

Poggio (*miming a hand-job*)
Funny, I thought you'd be helping him with his grip

Leonardo Oh no his hands are full with another Medici

Poggio Oh I am literally dying of curiosity

Sandro And I'll be literally dead if you gossip about it

Poggio Honey give me some credit I know what's off
limits

Sandro Well it's off limits
I have to play fucking squash with him in the morning

Poggio Well la-di-dah

Sandro Right

Poggio Is she naked?

Sandro turns and looks at him.

I heard you're painting her starkers

Sandro Who told you that?

Poggio Holy fuck – she is!

Sandro I'm neither confirming nor denying

Poggio Are you insane?
People are going to lose their minds

Sandro They'll be too busy trying to pick their jaws off
the ground

Poggio It's good?

Sandro Oh it's good

Poggio Really though?

Sandro Maybe the best

Poggio Oh honey you gotta show me the receipts
if you're going to say shit like that

He makes to get up.

Sandro Sit your ass down

Poggio You're kidding

Sandro Not until it's finished

Poggio Your best?

Sandro No
I mean the best ever

Poggio Oh that's sadistic

Sandro You'll make a bunch of snipy comments –

Poggio I won't!

Sandro   – and it'll mess me up

Poggio And after all the help I gave you with the
Primavera!

Sandro Please, when you saw it I had one figure left

Poggio And I was the one who told you you should
model him off Leo!

Sandro Oh wow I should give you half my commission

Poggio And now – yeah maybe you should
because now all everyone talks about is how fuckable
Mercury turned out!

Sandro I'm not showing you the canvas
Besides it'd be a breach of trust

Poggio Oh please you're painting her completely naked /
what's left to be breached?

Sandro I'm a man of honour

Poggio Hold on hold on what are we talking about here
are we talking –

*He makes a gesture for 'breasts'. Sandro is coy. Poggio
makes a gesture for 'vagina' and Sandro smiles.*

No

Sandro Well

Poggio Is it red?

Sandro makes exasperated gesture.

Oh don't think the entire city isn't wondering
about those carpet and drapes!

*Poggio jumps up and begins rushing towards the
canvas. Sandro jumps up and grabs him. They tumble
to the ground howling with laughter.*

Oooo I'm hurt

Sandro Shit did I fall on you?

Poggio No Sandro I'm your best friend
This is the biggest commission of your life your
whole life
and you won't even share it with me
not even a tiny little infinitesimal little fart of a peek

Sandro You're a little fart

Poggio It hurts me

Sandro A little queef, a little queer queef

Poggio I can't believe they trust you with royalty
You're a man child

*He suddenly palms a palette of paint and smears it
across Sandro's face, distracting him, and dashes to the
canvas. Poggio rips the tarp off the canvas and gasps.
The painting remains turned away from the audience.*

Ave, O Maria, piena di grazia

Sandro It's not finished

Poggio They're going to kill you
They're going to worship you
don't get me wrong
But they are going to kill you

Leonardo (*walks over and points to the painting*)
What do you think about the angle of her leg here?
Does something seem off about it?

*Poggio bursts out laughing. He turns to Sandro and
points at the painting.*

Poggio I really can't believe this
I mean nobody has done this since the Romans

Leonardo Not even

Poggio Sorry?

Leonardo Not even the Romans painted a nude of
this scale before

Poggio Seriously, are you trying to martyr yourself?
Do you realise – I mean it's fucking brilliant don't get
me wrong
but you do realise how many people this is going
to piss off, right?

Sandro Are you not moved?

Poggio Of course I am!
That's not the point!
Are you ready for the shit-storm?

Sandro When it's finished –

Poggio Sandro

Sandro – there'll be no denying its beauty

Poggio There's no denying it now
But beauty's not enough

Sandro covers the canvas with the tarp once more.

Sandro You see what I mean?

Poggio What?

Sandro You piss on whatever I'm working on

Poggio C'mon that's not what I was –

Sandro You do, you have no idea no fucking idea how
how delicate
how specific the alchemy of this is and how
you – / you just blunder in here and upset everything

Poggio You think you can paint the Medici's wife buck /
naked and not provoke –?

Sandro She is giving me permission to make myself
naked with her do you understand she is pushing
me inspiring me to unlock something in myself that
I mean you think the Vatican the fucking Church
would ever let me – this this is – ancient – this –

Poggio Sandro I don't want to lose you and that is why
I'm sitting here with you
drinking this shitty wine from Vinci that tastes like piss
(*Turns to Leonardo.*) no offence but I'm a connoisseur
and I don't mean of wine
sitting here as we bandage each other up

38

because who the hell knows when those assholes / will
    bust in here with –

Sandro Stop it

Poggio Stop what?
    It's already begun honey
    There're people in the piazza shouting 'Burn the
    sodomites!'

Sandro I know but –

Poggio I'll tell you what I know:
    they'll start with Verrocchio and his butt boys
    and then they'll come for Antonio and my fat ass –

Leonardo See?

Sandro C'mon

Poggio – and then they'll probably round off the cinders
    with Paulo de Sica!

Sandro Shut up
    Okay?
    You think this helps?
    Filling Leo's head with this bullshit?

Poggio And what about your head?
    It's so far up the Medici's ass you don't even realise
        how dark its gotten out here
    Not all of us can be the court fairy

Sandro Wow

Poggio Yes wow it's dark alright it's fucking bleak out
        there and you
    you've got to wake up to it because we all know
    The queens tell me you're too much of a big shot now
    You've forgotten about us
    Too busy fucking around with royalty
    and I stick up for you I stick up for you every time
    I don't mind being your poor sissy-ass friend babe

39

I don't mind being in your shadow
but do not forget who you are at the end of the day
Do not forget you are a worthless faggot
Just like the rest of us

Sandro Christians don't burn people

Poggio I'm sorry?

Sandro Say what you like about them
their politics their home decor their ridiculous
children's names they do not burn people
And you know why?
Because they've been burned
Romans used to burn Christians

Poggio Oh please –

Sandro Do you know how many of their martyrs were
burned on pyres?

Poggio Do you think any of those idiots out there in the
piazza is cracking open their codex and reading
about St Polycarp and Lucia?

*Sandro bursts out laughing. Then Poggio starts to
laugh.*

You brilliant idiots I love you so goddamn much

*Leonardo refills Poggio and Sandro's wine glasses. He
hands their glasses to them.*

Leonardo Don't you think it's funny
All those saints were burned for their love of a man
and now they want to burn us for the same thing

Sandro (*raises his glass*) St Poggio
Patron saint of sucking off married men in city parks

Poggio Yes and my holy relic will just be my withered
hand giving you the middle finger

They laugh.

Nel nome del Padre e del Figlio e dello Spirito Santo
    Amen

They all raise their glasses and toast.

Sandro, **Leonardo** *and* **Poggio** Amen

*Alternatively the three men may replace 'Amen' with
'Gay men'.*

Lights shift.

SIX

*A squash court at the Medici Palace. Sandro and
Lorenzo are in runners, T-shirts, shorts, and wearing
sweat bands around their foreheads. Clarice sits in a
lawn chair to the side, reading a magazine.*

Lorenzo We'll hang him

Clarice No
    No, no, no

Lorenzo Right in the fucking piazza where he preaches

Clarice You'll have an uprising
    He's baiting you, do you get that?
    And you can't bite
    You have to give the people a vision

Lorenzo I'm giving them the goddamn Renaissance
    what more do they fucking want?

Clarice People are scared, they're dying, they –

Lorenzo – want a miracle from the fucking sky and
    I don't have one

Clarice Well I might

Lorenzo Oh really?

Clarice Sewers

Lorenzo I'm sorry?

Clarice People are dumping their waste into the streets
and –

*Lorenzo begins laughing. He looks at Sandro, who
begins laughing too, unsure if that's the correct
response.*

– fleas are breeding there and spreading – why are you
laughing?

Lorenzo Savonarola is offering the people God and you
want to offer them sewers?

Clarice This is the single –

Lorenzo still laughing.

Lorenzo Oh yes I can see it now – Lorenzo the Effluent!
His father built the Basilica and he built a tunnel of
shit, how inspiring!
(*Turns to Sandro.*) You know all this is her fault in
the first place

Sandro Oh?

Clarice I swear to God if you say / that one more time

Lorenzo She begged me to bring him to Florence
She said he's a true prophet

Clarice No I offered him safe haven
It's a city of / free speech

Lorenzo I said fine, I'll indulge her
It was either that or a dachshund
and I've never really been one for small dogs

So we bring him to Florence
Right away he starts acting up
Ranting on the street corners
Blaming Clarice and me for all sorts of horrors, the
    ungrateful bastard
At first I think nothing of it
This city's full of crazies, / what's another?

Clarice He is not / just some crazy

Lorenzo First it's a crowd of eighty or a hundred
A few weeks later it's up to a thousand
His last sermon – if you can call it that
seven thousand people

Sandro Are you nervous?

Lorenzo Damn right I'm nervous
He's busting my fucking balls

Clarice Well in case you haven't noticed
there's a lot of sick and dying people and they want
    answers
and they're not happy with the answers Lorenzo has
    for them

Sandro But all this about being the fleas sucking the
    people's blood –

Clarice That's just rhetoric for the masses

Sandro Burn the sodomites?

Lorenzo The first time I met him I – (*Laughs.*)
I was giving him a tour of the San Marco convent
and this nun in a wheelchair coasted past us
and I said to him: 'Hey father, look: Virgin Mobile'
(*Bursts out laughing.*) He didn't get it
He has no sense of humour

Clarice Well ignore him at your peril
That's what I say

Lorenzo Oh is that what you say?
   Thanks for the support Clarice
   I'm not fucking ignoring him

Clarice You're dismissing him
   He's speaking to people's souls
   He's giving them hope and / you're dismissing him –

Lorenzo Fine but he's mostly speaking to the souls of
      the illiterate and ignorant
   I mean let's be honest / that's where most of his base
      seems to be

Clarice stands.

Clarice I'm tired of you patronising me

Lorenzo No one is –

Clarice (*To Sandro*)
   Lorenzo can't imagine why anyone would challenge
      him
   He doesn't believe in God but believes he has a /
      God-given right to power

Lorenzo He and his death cult want to take us back
      to the fucking Dark Ages

Clarice The friar is / speaking for the people
   He is giving them hope

Lorenzo Hatred of reason
   Hatred of liberty
   Hatred of sex
   Hatred of women
   Hatred of pleasure and desire
   Hatred of the self, of himself, I bet he does
   I bet he hates himself
   I sure the hell do

Clarice He believes in people's souls

Lorenzo He believes in dominance and submission

44

Clarice Please, you love dominance and submission

Lorenzo laughs.

The only thing you believe in is yourself

Lorenzo People have the right to do everything in their
   power
to achieve the greatest amount of pleasure possible
   to them
assuming –

Clarice makes to interrupt.

assuming
they don't infringe on the right of others to do the
   same
Simple as that

Clarice Oh is it?

Lorenzo Yes

Clarice Why don't you tell Mariana that?

Lorenzo Who?

Clarice Mariana

Lorenzo Who the fuck / is Mariana?

Clarice Our head maid for twelve years
   Her son just died of the plague
   We gave her flowers this morning

Lorenzo I would
   I would tell it to her face

Clarice Some people need an after-life Lorenzo
   because you've made this one unbearable for them

   She storms out.

Lorenzo It's nothing new, really
   My father dealt with the same thing

There's always a plague
There's always a fire
And there's always a friar who wants to throw things
    in it

*He takes out a hunting knife and cuts off a tag on his
sports bag with it.*

You following the play-offs?

Sandro Not really

Silence.

Lorenzo The markets?

Sandro You mean like – stocks?

Lorenzo They took a nosedive this morning
    Everyone's – jumpy

Sandro nods.

I trust you won't share that little episode
with your queers at some art party now

Sandro No, no (*Chuckles.*)

Lorenzo You can be a terrible gossip sometimes

*Sandro mimes zipping his lips, throwing away the
key – a little too eager to please.
    Lorenzo smiles, slaps Sandro's back and nods to the
squash court. Sandro clearly doesn't want to actually
play, but dutifully acquiesces.
    The two men play squash.
    Lorenzo decimates Sandro.
    Between rounds, Lorenzo grabs his water bottle and
shoots water into his mouth.*

Clarice makes me so – I'm not fucking ignoring –
There are a thousand doctors and nurses working
    round the clock right now
Why do you think we passed that emergency budget?

Sandro If the unrest gets worse –

Lorenzo Oh it's going to get worse, trust me
But we'll weather it
We always do

Sandro At the villa?

Lorenzo looks at Sandro and bursts out laughing.

Lorenzo You're such a little cunt

Sandro laughs too, uncertain if this is the correct response.
They resume the game.

We must have you back up there soon
I miss our walks together up there

Sandro Me too

Lorenzo We should go to the villa
I've just been so fucking busy
But we should, we should go to the villa
and go for one of our walks together
Nice bottle of wine, laugh around the fire

Sandro I would like that

Lorenzo And you can even bring your latest flavour
of the month, what's his name?

Sandro Leonardo's just my –

Lorenzo That's right, Leonardo
I can't keep track, you're so damn voracious

He wins that round, laughs and slaps Sandro on the back.

You're my only friend, you know that?

Sandro What?

Lorenzo You must know that

Sandro Well I –

Lorenzo You're the only person who doesn't want
        anything from me Sandro
    Everyone in the world they just –
    they just see what I can do for them
    But you – I can be real with you

Sandro I feel the same

Lorenzo Which
    means more to me these days than ever
    As you might imagine

Sandro Of course

Lorenzo You uh
    didn't reply to my text

Sandro Oh?

Lorenzo How's it coming?

Sandro The –

Lorenzo   – painting

Sandro It's great

Lorenzo Twenty sittings!

Sandro Yeah

Lorenzo Wow

Sandro Yeah

Lorenzo Is that usual?

Sandro Well –

Lorenzo What kind of painting requires twenty sittings?

Sandro A masterpiece

Lorenzo And is it?

Sandro There has never been a painting like it

Lorenzo You've outdone yourself

Sandro I . . . didn't hold back
Like you said

Lorenzo I did, didn't I, I said –

Sandro – don't hold back, so –

Lorenzo Well then I must come by your studio and
take a peek

Sandro A peek?

Lorenzo My curiosity is inflamed

Sandro It's uh it's still very much in process

Lorenzo Oh of course, I know
I'd just love to see how it's coming along
It's been a rather sizeable investment, after all

Sandro Right

Lorenzo Not least of which being my wife's time

Sandro She's been very – patient with me

Lorenzo I'll just pop by tomorrow morning

Sandro Tomorrow?

Lorenzo Morning yes, say around eleven?

Sandro Wow, well / um –

Lorenzo I trust that's alright

Sandro I'm afraid I have brunch plans –

Lorenzo Cancel them
We'll toast the masterpiece

Sandro I'm just a little – shy about where it's / at, it's –

Lorenzo Sandro, come
You know I won't judge
But it better be fucking great

Lorenzo points a finger at Sandro and then chuckles.
Sandro laughs, uncertain.
Clarice reappears.

Clarice I can't find my car keys

Lorenzo Where're you going?
We haven't even had breakfast

Clarice I'm upset
I need to go for a drive

Lorenzo What the hell are you / so upset about?

Clarice Where are my keys?

Lorenzo Besides you can't drive without a security
detail / you know that

Clarice Where are my fucking keys?

Lorenzo How the hell should I know?
Probably in that damn clam shell on the bookshelf

Clarice exits.

Lorenzo Mimosa?

Sandro No, I should be getting back
I have a lot of work to do

Lorenzo I love you like a brother, you know that?

Sandro You had your brother killed

Lorenzo I love you like the brother I never had and
never killed

He smiles, squeezes Sandro's shoulder.

Spotlight appears on Sandro.

Sandro I ran all the way home
   I could've had their driver take me
   But no   **Chorus**
   I needed to run   one-tenth
   I could've hailed a cab but I was
     already running   is a quarter
   It was raining   to the ears
   I thought: good, I'm glad it's raining   one-
   Rain is appropriate   seventh
   I ran through streets choked with
     protesters   of the face
   and I thought: good, I'm glad they're
     screaming   at half
   Someone should be screaming   eyes
                              knee
                              breasts
                              from below
                              one-third

                            Repeats softly
                            three times.

SEVEN

Sandro bursts into the studio.
   Leonardo is doing minor touch-ups on the 'Birth of Venus' canvas.

Sandro She needs longer hair

Leonardo What?

Sandro Her hair's gotta cover her vagina

Leonardo I spent a week on that vagina

Sandro And you did a very commendable job sweetie

for a man who's never seen one up close before
but the Medici's paying us a visit

Leonardo And?

Sandro I miscalculated

Leonardo You –

Sandro It was a test
That's it, isn't it, it was all a test to see if I would –
The commission
If Clarice and I would –

Leonardo What the hell are you saying?

Sandro And I failed, we failed

Leonardo But you knew he would see it

Sandro Yes I know I knew
But now
The details
It's too much

Leonardo But the nude was her idea

Sandro Yes yes she's testing him too and I'm right in
the fucking –
Leo I'm the only person in the world he thinks he
can trust
and he just –
He needed to know if he really could

They consider the canvas.

Leonardo Maybe he won't mind

Sandro It's smut

Leonardo Yeah he'll probably mind

Sandro Absolutely fucking brilliant smut

Leonardo Does he want to see it before the summer?

Sandro No sweetie, he's coming tomorrow morning

Leonardo What?

Sandro It's a nightmare, yes

Leonardo We could paint a dress over her

Sandro Don't be insane, that would completely destroy it

Leonardo Sandro

Sandro This is my masterpiece

Leonardo And you're prepared to go to jail for it?

Sandro If it comes to that

Leonardo You cry when you get paper cuts

Sandro This – this is my fucking soul

Leonardo Please

Sandro Every one of these paintings is a piece of my soul

Leonardo You're an atheist, you don't believe in souls

Sandro Exactly so what else is there?
Beauty
It's the only sacred thing

Leonardo The only thing sacred to you is your cock
And your genius, maybe

Sandro My genius –
You cannot *be* a genius
Beauty can only work through you
and holy shit she is working through me now, Leo
Venus alighting on the shore
the winds caressing her with a heavenly raiment
    of roses
It is the birth of love itself
It is working *through* me, Leo
like a direct line tapped right into the fucking cosmos
where no, there is no vengeful old god

where there is only sublime beauty and pleasure
And that is my duty
To defy ugliness and suffering
If I cannot live for at least that
then honestly? shoot me in the fucking face
This is bigger than me
And it's bigger than the Medici
We are not destroying this canvas
And we are not running away
At least I'm not and I hope to God you're with me

Leonardo (*beat*) I'm with you

Sandro Besides there's nothing about the painting that
     explicitly suggests I'm fucking his wife
(*Beat*). That said we should probably cover her vagina

Leonardo If we want to do it right it'll take days

Sandro We're doing it right

Leonardo But it's not just the hair I mean we have to
     move her entire left arm too
which then means repainting the entire raiment –

Sandro Leo

Leonardo There's just not enough time

Sandro Let me tell you what's going to happen
I'm going to open the Cabernet Sauvignon, alright
The *good* one
And you're going to mix me some ochre, cinnabar,
     red lake, and the purest virginal white
We're going to crack open the fresh brushes, put
     on some tunes
and we're not stopping until fucking daybreak, got it?

*He turns to get started, but turns back when he realises
Leonardo is still standing there.*

54

Sandro Honey
It's time to werk!

A nineties techno song begins to play as the men set to work.
Flower petals fall from the sky as Venus appears on a clam shell. She is singing the song, perhaps with the Chorus as backup dancers in gold lamé booty shorts. It is an explosive, flamboyant stage image.
Lights slowly fade on everything but Venus's face. The song dies away. Venus speaks.

Venus When I was a little girl everyone would say
Venus you are the most sublime creature to ever
walk the earth
And I said: cool thanks
They said: Venus your beauty outshines that of the sun
mortal men write poems and paint paintings in praise
of your divine perfection
And I said: yeah I know
They said: Venus we will make you the goddess of
love and beauty
and your name will be hallowed for all of eternity
And I said: you know what, you really don't need
to do that
The truth is I got bored of being beautiful, of beautiful
things
of beautiful men singing beautiful songs to me
As I grew up I wanted nasty-ass fuckers
I wanted men with crooked teeth and bent cocks
into dirty talk and piss play in cheap motels
I wanted to make love to subhumans, to Neanderthal
men
dragging their knuckles through dark back alleys
who could bite beer caps off bottles with their bare
teeth
and tell you the year and make of a car by the sound
of its engine

55

The worst, though, is being beautiful and young
    forever
Never getting fat, never getting wrinkled
never getting to feel the exquisite transcendence
    of death
Honestly?
I would trade beauty for death in a heartbeat

EIGHT

*Lights rise once again on Sandro's studio. The dead of
night. The two men frantically work to finish the canvas.*

Leonardo What is it?

Sandro Do you smell something?

Leonardo No

Sandro It's almost like –

Leonardo Fuck it's already midnight

Sandro Open the window

Leonardo What?

Sandro Just open the window

Leonardo gets up and opens the window.

Leonardo Whoa yeah I can sm—
Sandro

*In the darkness we hear the voices of two Boys,
singing, unseen.*

Boy 1	**Boy 2**
And, lo, the smoke	And, lo, the smoke of the country
the smoke	

And, lo, the smoke of the
    country /   went up
as the smoke of a furnace
And, lo, the smoke   And, lo, the smoke
And the Lord rained   And the Lord rained upon
                        Sodom
And, lo, the smoke /   and upon Gomorrah
the smoke of the
    country went up /   brimstone and fire out of heaven
        lo, the smoke / and he overthrew those cities
And all the plain   And all the plain
And, lo, the smoke   And all the inhabitants of the
                      cities
                  and that which grew
upon the ground   upon the ground
And, lo, the smoke /   of the country went up
as the smoke of a furnace

Sandro goes over to the window. Spotlight appears. He speaks to the audience.

Sandro In the distance, smoke was rising from the piazza
It was the dead of night
but the flames lit the black plume from below
From where we stood we could not see the pyre
or the gathered mob
but we knew
It had started

Leonardo Are they – ?

Sandro Yes

Leonardo That smell –

Sandro It's flesh

Leonardo The smell of burning –

Sandro Faggots

Leonardo retches.

Leonardo It's in my throat

Sandro Just stay calm

Leonardo You said the earth was round

Sandro Leo

Leonardo You said this was the fucking Renaissance

Sandro Leo listen to me

Leonardo We're fucked

Sandro No

Leonardo You're the most flagrant sodomite in Florence
     they're probably building your pyre as we speak

Sandro That is not constructive thinking

Leonardo We're so fucked

Sandro We are not / fucked, we just –

Leonardo We bet on the wrong horse

Sandro The Medici have an army
     They have allies

Leonardo We need to get out of here

Sandro What's this 'we'?
     You can go whenever you want
     I'll release you
     What are you even worried about?
     (*Points out of the window.*) This?
     Why should you get caught up in any of this?

Leonardo Just come with me

Sandro And go where?
     Run back to your mother's farm?

Leonardo Why not?

Sandro And wallow with the pigs?
  Eat turnips until our teeth fall out?

Leonardo Better than getting them fucking / knocked
  out by a mob

Sandro If I run away I have nothing –

Leonardo Sandro

Sandro – I'm less than nothing

Leonardo This is fucking madness

Sandro That mob is not the whole city

Leonardo It doesn't matter

Sandro There are still more reasonable people in / this
  city than not and together –

Leonardo It doesn't matter! Where are they?!

Sandro – we are bigger than madness and we will not
  be afraid –

Leonardo But I am / I'm afraid

Sandro – and we will live however the fuck we want

Leonardo You think they won't throw your ass on the fire
  because you can paint a few beautiful paintings?

Sandro The Medici are not going to let an angry mob /
  of of of fucking peasants –

Leonardo You don't get it do you?
  You're just another happy-go-lucky queer
  A real *delight* to have around
  Always a good quip, real life of the party
  You're a prestige item for them Sandro
  Like a . . . a fancy armoire

And lucky you you've gained a bit of power
But don't forget you're a happy-go-lucky queer
We're as disposable as lap dogs

Sandro Where's my phone?

Leonardo What?

Sandro My phone

Leonardo How can you –?

Sandro Just help me find it!

Leonardo realises what Sandro's thinking. He dashes over to the pile of sheets on the floor and finds the phone.

Leonardo Here I –

He glances down at the phone and cups his mouth.

Sandro What?
What is it?

A faint spot up on Poggio's face. Sandro crosses to Leonardo and looks at the phone.

Poggio Ten forty-nine
Missed call

Ten fifty
Missed call

Ten fifty
Missed call

Ten fifty-one
Turn on your phone girl
Bad news brewing

Ten fifty-three
Missed call

Ten fifty-seven
Shit's going down answer your fucking phone

Chorus begin slamming faggots of wood into giant pile at the centre of the stage.

Eleven
Missed call

Chorus
one
seventh
of a man

Eleven
Missed call

is

Eleven
Missed call

equal to the
head
and

Eleven o-two
Missed call

knee

Eleven o-two
Missed call

below the knee
is a quarter
is a half

Eleven o-four
For the love of God pick up pick
up pick up

Repeating.

Eleven o-four
Missed call

Eleven o-four
Missed call

Eleven o-five
Love you

Sandro *and* **Leonardo** (*murmur*)
Love you

Sandro breaks down in a fit of grief. He runs to the window sobbing. Leonardo restrains him. Sandro grows increasingly hysterical until there is a pounding at the door. They fall silent. The pounding comes again, this time louder. The two men hold each other, weeping.

Poggio (*offstage*) Open up you fuckers I know you're
in there

*Sandro is in disbelief. Leonardo jumps up and runs to
the door.*
Poggio stumbles in. He is a ghost of himself.
*Sandro runs to Poggio and hugs him as if he has
come back from the dead.*
After a long moment Sandro pulls away.

Sandro Who are they?

Poggio I don't know yet
But at least I can strike you two fuckers off the list

He makes to leave.

Sandro Whoa whoa whoa where're you going?

Poggio Girl you ain't my only friend

Sandro You can't go back out there

Poggio Verrocchio's not replying to my texts

*Sandro covers his mouth and nods, trying to contain
himself. He hugs Poggio one last time.*

Sandro Be careful

Poggio No
The time for being careful's over

Poggio exits.
*Sandro and Leonardo are left together in a moment
of silence, staring at one another.*

Leonardo I wish you would just fucking hold me for
a second

*Sandro comes up behind Leonardo and embraces him,
tentative at first, but then with greater insistence.
Something in them releases. Leonardo turns around
and kisses Sandro. The two men make out with a
passionate, almost agonised frenzy, as if this might be*

the last pleasure they ever feel. As the lights fade, they
strip one another bare.
    Spotlight up on the face of Maria.

Maria *(spoken softly and swiftly, underscoring)*
    the length of the outspread arms is equal to the
        height of a man
    from the hairline to the bottom of the chin is one-tenth
        of the height of a man
    from below the chin to the top of the head is one-eighth
        of the height of a man
    from above the chest to the top of the head is one-sixth
        of the height of a man
    from above the chest to the hairline is one-seventh
        of the height of a man
    the maximum width of the shoulders is a quarter
        of the height of a man
    from the breasts to the top of the head is a quarter
        of the height of a man
    the distance from the elbow to the tip of the hand
        is a quarter of the height of a man
    the distance from the elbow to the armpit is one-eighth
        of the height of a man
    the length of the hand is one-tenth of the height of
        a man
    the root of the penis is at half the height of a man
    the foot is one-seventh of the height of a man
    from below the foot to below the knee is a quarter
        of the height of a man
    from below the knee to the root of the penis is
        a quarter of the height of a man
    the distances from below the chin to the nose and
        the eyebrows and the hairline are equal to the ears
        and to one-third of the face

During Maria's text, the lights slowly fade to black.

End of Act One.

Act Two

Darkness.

Chorus one-tenth
    to the root
    of a man
    is a quarter
    to the top
    of the height
    top
    one-third

    eyes
    knee
    breasts

    from above
    is a quarter
    chin to the nose
    chin
    chin to the nose
    chin

    one-seventh
    top of the head
    of the face
    from below
    one third

    is a half
    top of the head
    top
    one

to the root
chin

equal to the ears
equal to the
nose

to the root
one-third
at half

one
tenth
of a man

from above
is a quarter
chin to the nose
chin
chin to the nose
chin

is a half
top of the head
top
one

*During this choral sequence the lights raise faintly on
Sandro's studio. Leonardo is asleep, still naked, while
Sandro frantically works on the canvas in his underwear.
A loud knocking. Sandro bolts upright.*

Sandro You gotta be fucking joking

Leonardo goes to the window and looks out.

Leonardo Here we go

Sandro Already?

Leonardo Black limo

Sandro Fuck

*Sandro throws a cloth over the painting. They both
flash about for a minute, frantically dressing.
Leonardo turns the canvas and easel around to face
the audience.*
   More knocking.

Leonardo Just get the door

Sandro Alright, alright just pick up this shit

Leonardo Pants!

Sandro You get the door!

   More knocking.

Leonardo For fuck's sake –

   *Leonardo exits to open the door.
      Sandro pulls his pants on.
      Clarice and Lorenzo enter, Leonardo trailing them.*

Lorenzo Sandro!
   I'm so excited I haven't slept a wink

Sandro Me neither

   *Sandro crosses to embrace Lorenzo. He makes to
   embrace Clarice but ends up awkwardly shaking her
   hand. Lorenzo bursts out laughing.*

Lorenzo (*chuckling*) Look at you two
   Like you're meeting for the first time

Sandro Would you like some coffee?

Lorenzo I don't drink coffee

Sandro Of course
   I knew that
   Like I said, I haven't slept

Lorenzo No sleep, no sleep for anyone
   Did you know them?
   The three men they burned?

Sandro Three

Lorenzo I wondered if they might be pals of yours from
  art school

Sandro What were their names?

Lorenzo I don't know, but we drove past on the way here
  Those fuckers smashed the back window
  Did I already mention that?

Sandro No

Lorenzo We're still a little shaken up

Clarice Can we make this quick?
  I have a headache

Lorenzo Can you give me fifteen minutes?
  In my whole goddamn day?
  This is my life these days Sandro
  Five minutes for breakfast
  Fifteen minutes for a friend
  And then putting out fires till bedtime
  Where's the fun? There's no time
  So I assume it's that one over there?

Lorenzo crosses to the canvas.

Lorenzo May I?

Sandro Before you do I just –

Lorenzo pulls off the cloth that covers it.
    *The canvas is revealed in its full glory for the first
time in the play. It is luminous.*
    Silence.

Clarice Well?
  What do you think?

Pause.

Do you like it?

67

Pause.

Lorenzo Wow

Clarice I told you it's a little bit daring

Lorenzo I uh . . .
Wow

Clarice (*to Sandro*)
I see you've taken a little creative liberty with the hair

Lorenzo I can see why it has taken a lot of sittings
It's . . . a masterpiece

Sandro A –?
You mean you –?
(*Laughing.*) Jesus, I can't tell you how nervous I was
for you to see it
I, I literally didn't sleep / a wink last night

Lorenzo I mean I can practically smell her she's so alive

Sandro Really

Lorenzo Do you know the smell I mean?
The earthy one
Like moss after a warm rain
With traces of talcum powder
Just looking at this painting I can smell it

Clarice I told you
It's a masterpiece

Lorenzo (*to Sandro*) Do you know the smell I mean?

Sandro Can't say I do

Lorenzo It's the funniest thing
Seeing you like this

Clarice Naked?

Lorenzo So . . . content

Clarice I'm always content

Lorenzo Those eyes
    I haven't seen those eyes in years

Clarice Don't be ridiculous
    You see me every day

Sandro It's funny, I was worried she looked bored in
        the painting
    (*Forced laughter.*) I mean after sitting for so long

Lorenzo (*to Clarice*) Can I ask you a favour?

Clarice Of course you / can ask –

Lorenzo Lie down on your back

Clarice (*chuckling*) What?

Lorenzo You heard me

Clarice . . .

Lorenzo I'm not going to ask you again

Clarice Why do you want / me to lie down on –?

Lorenzo Funny, that's exactly what I remember
    Even though it's been years

Clarice Lorenzo

Lorenzo The way you rest your hand like that over
        your breast
    with your fingers gently splayed above the other breast
    That's how you used to rest your hand when you're
        lying on your back, see
    That's always how you rested your hand
    always your right hand, just like that
    after we fucked
    Looking into each other's eyes
    Isn't that funny?

That I should see that hand here again
The first time in . . . oh, what . . . four years
Did she tell you this is how we lay together, Sandro
After we fucked
Her fingertips resting just above her left breast
How sweet of her to remember
how incredibly sexy and sentimental of her to relay
    this little gesture
Perhaps to rekindle the old fires, was that it sweetie?
Or perhaps, Sandro, you happened to find yourself
    sketching my wife naked and on her back
Somehow, and I can't imagine how
splayed like this in perfect simulation of post-coital
    bliss

Sandro If I may –

*Lorenzo punches Sandro in the face, knocking him
to the ground. Clarice screams and sits bolt upright.
Sandro's nose gushes blood.*

Lorenzo (*pointing at Leonardo*) You –
Fetch some ice

*Leonardo and Sandro glance at one another, and in
that brief instant something passes between them.
Clarice notices this. Leonardo runs out of the studio.
    Lorenzo pulls out his hunting knife.*

You know what I'd love, as your patron?
A peek at the great artist in action
Why don't you two pretend like I'm not here
(*Beat.*) Well – what are you waiting for?

Clarice Lorenzo –

Lorenzo Go on: fuck each other
Just pretend I'm not here

Sandro and Clarice do nothing.

Lorenzo I said –

Lorenzo lunges at Sandro. They scuffle. Clarice intercedes.

Did you think this was a game of squash?
Did you think my wife was a little ball you could
　　slam around the court?
A game you could beat me at and we'd pat each other
　　on the back
and go for a cold beer afterwards?

Clarice Fuck you
Do not scrutinise me and do not –
You think this is about you this is not about you
I am finally living and you can't stand it can you?

Lorenzo (*turns to Sandro*) And what about you?
You love her?

Sandro No

Lorenzo (*to Sandro*)
Our hunting trips, everything I confided
When you twisted your ankle in Umbria
I carried you two hours *two hours* on my back
What was that?
I fucking loved I fucking trusted you I wanted to but
　　I didn't and that's –
That's – (*Pointing at his chest.*)
Do you know what I have in mind for you?
There is a windowless cell in the basement of my
　　palace
with three feet of fetid water with pieces of shit
　　bobbing in it
because this is where the latrines of the palace empty
　　into, you see
like a sewer (*Glancing at Clarice.*)
and I'm thinking:

71

how delightful it will be to hear your moans and
    screams every time I take a shit
to open the toilet seat and shout down at you in the
    pitch dark
and even long after you're dead and your corpse is
    devoured by the rats
and just your white bones are left bobbing in the water
I'll shout down 'Good day friend, how's the weather
    down there?!'

Clarice Lorenzo –

Lorenzo Shut up

Sandro If I / might –

Lorenzo Did I say you could speak?
    Put your mouth around my shoe
    Go on, bite my shoe

*Sandro slowly gets to his knees and puts his mouth
around Lorenzo's shoe.*

Snakes can't help their nature, can they?
They eat whatever hot-blooded thing they can get
    their mouths around
And yet sticking you down my toilet feels somehow . . .
    anticlimactic doesn't it?
For a man of so many climaxes like yourself
It almost seems more fitting – an almost Biblical
    judgement
To cut off the evil at the root of the problem
Get up

*He gives his foot a kick causing Sandro to exclaim in
pain. Sandro stands, his mouth bleeding.*

Lorenzo Pull down your pants

Clarice Lorenzo stop it

Lorenzo I said pull down your pants!

Sandro pulls down his pants.

Do you have . . . an erection?

Sandro I'm sorry, I –

Lorenzo Even now, you have a fucking erection?

Sandro One final salute I suppose

Lorenzo I am doing you a favour I hope you realise

Sandro I'm sure I'll see it that way one day

Lorenzo Take it out

Clarice Stop

Lorenzo Clarice for / fuck sake –

Clarice I swear to God I'll smash every window
  in every car and house you own

Lorenzo He . . . you . . . have *hurt* me

Clarice So you want to hurt him?

Lorenzo I want –

Clarice To punish him?

Lorenzo Yes

Clarice Then take away the thing he loves

Lorenzo What do you think I'm doing?

Clarice Take the boy

Sandro What?

Clarice He loves the boy
  So take something from him
  Better yet
  Buy some favour with the masses

Turn the boy over to the Friar as the sodomite he is
Look! they'll say
The Medici clean house!

Lorenzo (*to Sandro*)
You see how my wife bargains with me?
She does this with everything
I want a black leather couch, she wants the white one
She'll say – (*To Clarice.*) do you remember?
'If we get the white couch
you can have the granite counter top in the en-suite'
What do you say to that?

Sandro doesn't answer.

Is the boy your peace offering?

Sandro doesn't answer. Lorenzo presses the knife up to Botticelli's groin.

Lorenzo Speak up   **Sandro** (*whispers/gasps*)
                                        Yes

Pardon?

Sandro Yes

Lorenzo (*to Clarice*) You get your white couch

He takes out a cell phone and dials a number.

Yes, waylay the boy on his return
Leonardo
Yes
Put him in the toilet

He puts away his phone.

Well I must be going
Sorry for the short visit
Oh and – (*Referring to the canvas.*) no rush on
    finishing that up
I'm not sure we have room for it anyway

Lorenzo makes to leave.

Sandro Can I see him?

Lorenzo Well of course you can
They burn them in public

Lorenzo exits.
    *Sandro and Clarice are alone in the studio for a
moment.*
    Clarice exits.
    *For a long moment Sandro does nothing. Then he
throws a fit. He smashes a chair, he tears off his
clothes. He trashes his studio.*
    *The Chorus begin singing the madrigal from the top
of the show.*
    *Naked, Sandro begins throwing paint at the 'Birth
of Venus' until it resembles a Jackson Pollock abstract.*
    Blackout.

TWO

Darkness.
    *A faint spotlight appears on Leonardo's face. He is
naked, shivering, and his hands are handcuffed together.
He is seated on the ground, as if in a prison cell.*

Leonardo Dear God, if I'm a sodomite, what are you?
If you made me in your image
and I'm an abomination, what are you?
If I'm a sodomite, what are you God?
And where is my town
if you destroyed Sodom in a rain of fire
A stealth bomber over the desert
breaking the sound barrier
What are you if not a gravedigger?
If not a psychopath in the desert
If I am a sodomite, what the fuck are you?

What are you?
If I am, then what are you
If I am God
then what is
If I am
What is
If I am
I am
If I am
I am
I am
I am

THREE

Lights rise on Sandro's studio. He is drunk and has passed out, surrounded by half-empty wine bottles.

Maria enters. She takes in the ravaged studio and rushes over to Sandro. She tries to rouse him, but to no avail. She walks over to the work bench, grabs a small basin and a cloth, exits offstage, and returns with the basin filled with water.

She proceeds to dump the basin of water over Sandro's head. He bolts upright, gasping.

Maria begins stripping off Sandro's shirt.

Maria You're a mess

Sandro Jesus Christ what the / hell are you doing?

Maria Have you pissed yourself?

Sandro Just –

Maria removes Sandro's shirt and begins trying for his pants.

Maria Baby you should have called me

Sandro They took Leonardo

Maria stops.

And I let them
They came and I just –

Gestures as if to say 'I just gave him away'.
Maria continues undressing Sandro, pulling off his
pants.

Sandro Ma would you just –

Maria They reek
Take them off

Sandro Do you think I care about –?

Maria (*snaps her fingers*) Off

Botticelli removes his pants. And begins to cry.
Maria leaves with the clothes and the washbasin.
She returns with the washbasin, once again filled with
water, but this time sudsy. She holds a sponge.

You let company use that washroom?
With pubes all over the toilet seat like that?

Sandro Ma

Maria holds Sandro in a position resembling the Pietà.
She begins bathing him with the sponge.

Ah ah ah ah that's cold

Maria It'll wake you up

She bathes Sandro for a few moments.

I knew something was wrong
I was dead asleep and I sat up and I knew I just
I sensed it

Sandro If you keep saying witchy shit like that they'll
burn you too

77

Maria I'd like to see them try

They laugh.
  Beat.

He's something special, isn't he?

Sandro nods.

So what are you going to do?

Sandro It's too late

Maria If you think like that

Sandro I lost him

Maria When you were a teenager you started bringing
  boys and girls home to bed
Sometimes three or four at a time, remember?
And oh the noise you would all make!
And look I gave a few winning blow jobs in my time
but you were out of control!
The neighbours would glare at me from behind their
  curtains
I cried to my priest: 'Father, what should I do?'
He said: 'You must show him the path; you must
  change his heart.'
But I said 'Oh, you don't know my Sandro, there's no
  changing him'
He came out of the womb sucking his own cock
Well I didn't tell the priest that, but it's true

Sandro I know

Maria The priest told me I had a choice to make
  'You can either continue to love this hopeless
    blasphemer
  or you can pour your love into God'
  And that's when I realised I loved God
  But I loved my baby more

I loved God – but I loved you more
I chose you
And I never went back
And now you have to choose
between love and your God

Sandro C'mon, you know I don't believe in God

Maria The thing you worship

Sandro What are you / talking about?

Maria You know exactly what I'm talking about

Beat.

The time has come, Sandro
You have to make a choice

Lights shift.

FOUR

Lights faintly rise again on Sandro's studio.
Sandro, dressed in a different shirt from earlier, busies himself trying to restore some semblance of order to the chaotic space. He scoops up an armful of wine bottles and exits into the next room with them to throw them out.

Poggio (*from offstage*) Hello?
Anybody?

He enters the studio, dressed as a nun. He surveys the damaged studio.

Oh my God

Sandro re-enters and screams when he sees Poggio.

It's just me girl
Oh babe

Poggio holds him.

Sandro They –

Poggio I know
I heard

Sandro pulls away.

Sandro What the hell's with the nun drag?

Poggio Honey those bastards can spot a sodomite a mile
away
What'd you think they'll do if they see my flaming
ass running through the streets?

Sandro (*holding the hem of Poggio's habit*)
How'd you even get this?

Poggio Oh I've had it for years
I've worn it to parties, you've seen me
I stole it when Verrocchio and I were painting that
fresco in Pistoia

Sandro Verrocchio, is he –?

Poggio They roughed him up pretty bad

Sandro No

Poggio He's okay for now but they'll come back for him
They're coming for all of us
(*Takes out a black robe for Sandro.*)
Look that's why I got you one of these sinister-ass
robes

Sandro You can't / be serious

Poggio And there's no way you're leaving here without it
Everyone in the city knows your face

Sandro I can't leave

Poggio Sandro

Sandro I'm getting him back

Poggio I know I know babe, and we will, but I'm here
to tell you –
while you've been fucking around with the Medici
Antonio and I've been hatching a plan to save our
sorry asses, alright?

Sandro That's great, really, but it's too / late for me,
I've already –

Poggio Anyone we think's a target we're getting them
to five different safe-houses across the city
A rich old client of mine from Arezzo's sending cars
to each of the houses
They're picking us up tonight at ten o'clock sharp,
alright
and we've / gotta be ready for them when they show

Sandro Babe I wish I could but I can't

Poggio I know you want to save Leo but if we try to
bust him out now we could blow the whole plan /
and then everyone's fucked

Sandro I don't have time to go / to Arezzo with you
and every queen in the city

Poggio Once we're at the safe-house we can / coordinate
from there

Sandro You need to go

Poggio I know and those fuckers could be back at any
minute
so just put on this fucking death frock and let's get
outta here

He begins trying to dress Sandro in the black robe.

Sandro No, no you have to go *now*

Poggio I know fuck and I'm trying to / take you with me –

Sandro Right now just go please, you / need to get out of here

Poggio – and every goddamn second we waste licking our wounds –

Sandro You don't understand I –

Savonarola appears in the doorway.

Poggio – risks fucking up everything, the entire plan, and there's a lot more –

He turns around, sees Savonarola, and screams.

Fuckfuckfuck it's too late!

Sandro Just, listen to me –

Poggio (*screaming at Savonarola*)
Get out of here get the fuck out of here you think we're afraid of you / you piece of shit get *out*

Sandro Poggio

Poggio (*to Savonarola*)
Don't move don't you take a single fucking step closer you hear

Sandro Listen

Savonarola Botticelli I suggest you get your barking guard dog under control

Sandro (*to Poggio*) I invited him

Poggio What?

Beat.

Sandro I need to get Leo back

Poggio Uh huh

Beat.

Sandro You have to understand –

Poggio Oh I understand things perfectly thank you
     very much

Beat.

This is some majorly fucked-up Faustian shit

Sandro Babe

Poggio Don't 'babe' me
     You're selling us out

Sandro I'm just trying to –

Poggio Don't you get it?
     When you sell out to him you sell us all out

Sandro I'm sorry

Poggio I will hide
     But I will not grovel
     Goodbye Sandro

*He exits, making a wide arch around Savonarola as he
goes.
     Sandro tries to call after Poggio but there is nothing
left to say.
     Silence.*

Sandro Can I get you something to drink?

Savonarola No

Sandro Camomile tea perhaps?

Savonarola (*taking in studio*)
     So this is where it all happens
     Your *genius*
     (*Points to the 'Birth of Venus' canvas.*)
     What on earth happened to this one?

Sandro It's a new style I'm toying with

Savonarola Huh

Sandro I didn't know if my message would reach you

Savonarola Yes
Well
I have to admit I was pleasantly surprised to receive
    your invitation
I was wondering when I would have the pleasure

Sandro I can't imagine you've had much in your life

Savonarola smirks, in spite of himself.

Savonarola Is it true what they say?
That you've had a thousand lovers

Sandro Mmm . . . I think you might have an old source

Savonarola And does this give your life meaning?
This wanton pursuit of flesh?
Seems rather bereft

Sandro And how about burning people?
That really gets you out of bed in the morning, huh?

Savonarola I'm as upset by the burnings as you are

Sandro Oh really?
Well lucky for you, last time I checked they were
    burning faggots, not friars

Savonarola And how long before the wind changes
    direction and we're all consumed by the fires?
You have me all wrong if you think I want to see
    anyone burned

Sandro But you are fanning the flames

Savonarola This is the people's revolution

Sandro Which you started

Savonarola The Medici brought this upon themselves
And I'm sorry if you happen to be collateral / in this
but –

Sandro They are burning faggots in Piazza del Signoria
because of your sermons

Savonarola I never told anyone / to burn anyone

Sandro The city is sick with the / pestilence of sin

Savonarola Yes, but I never –

Sandro And like Sodom and Gomorrah, its day of
reckoning is near!

Savonarola Do you berate all your guests like this?
You invited me over, I am a very busy man.

Sandro I know, I –

Savonarola Do I want you to burn on the pyre, of
course not
Do I want to save the souls of this city, yes
And I believe they can be, every last one of them
None of us are beyond redemption
Not even you

Sandro Spare Leonardo

Savonarola Remind me, which / one is he –?

Sandro The boy being held in the Medici's toilet

Savonarola Right

Sandro Collect Leonardo from the Medici and let him go
I'm begging you

Savonarola The people want a burning

Sandro If you could just reason with them

Savonarola You can't reason with a mob

Sandro You have influence
  They listen to you

Savonarola Botticelli –

Sandro Tell me what you want
  I can make it worth your while

Savonarola Are you bargaining with me?

Sandro I know how the world works

Savonarola But do you understand how God works?

Sandro If there is a God he will spare Leonardo

  Beat.

  Tell me what you want

  Pause.

Savonarola I want you to publicly denounce the Medici

Sandro Done

Savonarola And burn your paintings

Sandro Burn –

Savonarola Your entire studio
  Offer each and every one of your paintings to the
    bonfire

Sandro But –

Savonarola And then, Botticelli, you will renounce
    painting altogether
  and pledge your allegiance to my cause

Sandro When you say 'renounce' –?

Savonarola Throw every one of your brushes
  every pot of paint and canvas you own into the fire

You will publicly pledge to never paint again for as
    long as you live
Renounce your ways
Renounce all vice
and declare you have seen the light
This is a trade I would consider
If the greatest sinner of all can be saved in front of
    the masses
then anything is possible

*Sandro paces the studio, taking in each one of his
canvases as if his children.*
    A long, anxious, ruminating silence.

And in exchange I'll spare the boy

Sandro is silent. Agonised.
    He wrestles with the fate of his soul.
    Time passes.

I suggest you make up your mind quickly

Through tears, Sandro turns to Savonarola and smiles.

Sandro Burn them

Savonarola Burn them?

Sandro Burn all of them

Savonarola You want to / burn them?

Sandro I want to . . . to . . . throw them into the fucking
    fire

Savonarola I see

Sandro Just give me a stick and some marshmallows

Savonarola That's quite the about-face

Sandro I have – seen the light

    Savonarola points his finger at Sandro, thinking.

Savonarola It's good
  It's a good start
  But uh –
  Still
  I'm not quite sure it's –

Sandro Enough?

Savonarola Well it doesn't really have the same impact
    does it?
  A few paintings
  The people have come to expect a certain –
  I'm just not sure it drives home the point in quite the
    same way

Sandro Then burn more

Savonarola More?

Sandro Everything
  Every occasion of sin

Savonarola Oh?

Sandro Books
  For instance

Savonarola Books?

Sandro Musical instruments and and and sheet music

Savonarola Yes

Sandro Porn, cosmetics, jewels, uh uh fancy dresses

Savonarola The Greek manuscripts

Sandro All the heretical writings

Savonarola Yes yes

Sandro Costumes and masks

Savonarola Tapestries

Sandro People could offer up their own possessions

Savonarola Self-elected

Sandro A, a, a great purging!

Savonarola Fed by the flames of your paintings

Sandro Just – use them as kindling

Savonarola A great bonfire

Sandro A bonfire of the vanities

Savonarola Yes
Yes yes yes
Or what if we called it –?
No that's good
A Bonfire of the Vanities
Tomorrow at sunrise you will throw your paintings
on to the pyre

Sandro Every one

Savonarola (*pointing to the destroyed 'Birth of Venus'
canvas*) Except that one, that's a piece of shit

Sandro In exchange for Leonardo

Savonarola What?
Oh yes . . . I'll see what I can do

Blackout.

FIVE

*A deep rumbling. The rumbling begins to deepen, grows
louder, becomes something verging on the tectonic, like
the sound of the earth rupturing.*
    A bonfire blazes.

Chorus 1	Chorus 2
the arms	
	one-tenth
the chin	one-eighth
the head	
	one-sixth
the chest	one-seventh
the hairline	a quarter
the shoulders	
the eyebrows	
the breasts	
the elbow	
	one-eighth
the armpit	a quarter
the hand	
the penis	one-seventh
the foot	
the knee	
	a quarter
the chin	
the nose	one-third
the ears	

Repeating softly.   *Repeating softly.*

Sandro appears, holding several of his canvases. His silhouette looms large in the blaze of the fire.
    Sounds of a crowd, cheering.
    Sandro is silent for a moment, steeling himself. He picks up a microphone attached to an amp; the same used by Savonarola in Act One.

Sandro I wanted to say
    If I might . . .
    There was once a great fire within me
    But I have come to realise that my paintings are . . .
    nothing
    but sinful, earthly distractions

I mean look at this one
Pure pagan propaganda
(*Indicates a painting.*) Nothing but flesh
I never noticed how gauzy those gowns were
Do they need to be so . . . sheer and sensuous?
I mean her breasts are basically pouring out
And look: Mercury is barely wearing that sheet
He's on full display
Yeah, there's no denying it, it's just a garden of flesh
(*Turns to another painting.*) And my God where do I
    even start with this one?
Those cherubs . . . are clearly devils
The horns, the cloven hooves
Those little devil lips blowing into Mars's ear
makes him throw his head back in ecstasy – he's spent
The jugular exposed
We follow that line, which leads us down his perfectly
    taut chest
Past his jutting hip
All the way to his hand, clearly indicating the main
    focus of the painting
clearly positioned as if holding an imaginary cock
Like if you squint it's like he's holding his cock
It's all so obvious
(*Turns to another painting.*) Even the religious ones –
    look
St Sebastian, pierced by arrows – why does he look
    orgasmic?
And this one
The Virgin Mary
The Mother of God
And her nipples are erect?
Her nipples are erect!
Like who did I think I was fooling?
Forgive me
For giving life to these visions

By my hand they were born
And by my hand they will die

The roar of the flames and the crowd climax.
  Blackout.

The choral madrigal from the top of the show resumes.
Faces appear, faintly illuminated in the dark.

Maria We walked home in silence

Clarice What became of Botticelli?

Savonarola He had a crisis of faith

Maria And he didn't cry

Clarice Stopped painting, as far as I know

Poggio I don't want to hear that name

Clarice He faded into obscurity

Lorenzo Florence was blue-balled for years after

Savonarola Consider for a moment, if you will –

Maria I tied his hands to the bars of the crib

Savonarola – what we were trying to achieve

Clarice I prefer not to think about it

Lorenzo I mean it's nothing really new, is it?
  There's always a plague
  There's always a fire

Poggio Ave, O Maria, piena di grazia

Maria I loved him like any mother

Clarice I said I prefer not to think about it

Lights up faintly on Sandro's studio. It is completely bare except for the 'Birth of Venus' canvas, propped up against the back wall. The 'Jackson Pollock-style' paint splatters have mostly been wiped away, revealing much of the completed canvas below. He sits alone for a long moment in silence.

Sandro (*to audience*)
    You can't possibly hate me more than I hate myself
    So save your judgement
    I don't need your pity either
    You might be watching this and thinking:
    well obviously the Medici were going down
    Obviously Florence would fall to the zealots
    Nah uh, take it from me –
    it's not as easy to tell when you're on the precipice
        as you might think
    We convince ourselves things will more or less stay
        the course
    That progress is a forward –

Leonardo, gaunt and damp, enters.
    Sandro leaps to his feet but Leonardo takes a step back. He does not want to be touched. A moment of silence.

Leonardo Don't –

Beat.

I thought you were –

Beat.

When they let me out I ran to the piazza
I saw what was left of the fire and I –
I really thought that you were –

He coughs up some blood.

Sandro You must be starving
Do you want me to make / you something to eat?

Leonardo I came for my backpack. Have you seen it
around?

Sandro does a cursory scan of the empty room.

Sandro No

Leonardo Fuck
Had my passport in it

Pause.

Are we all just playthings to you?
Huh?
Cum rags to keep you company?
Things to keep around to laugh at your jokes
fawn over your genius
and then fuck every once and a while
and then put back in the cupboard?
Or do you fuck because you can no longer feel love
just cheap sensation?
Frankly, I think you've forgotten how to love anything
but yourself
You find no human quite so alluring as your own genius
so we'll just have to be your disposable substitutes
until you do

Sandro I'm sorry

Leonardo You're sorry

Sandro I burned everything for you

Leonardo begins a slow clap for him.

Leonardo Go suck a bag of dicks

He turns to go.

Sandro Wait
Where will you go?

Leonardo I'll find my way

Sandro Please just –

Leonardo coughs up more blood.

Leonardo The palace is empty

Sandro And the Medici –?

Leonardo Fled, yes
Or perhaps they're just on vacation

Beat.

And look – I guess they left their fancy armoire behind

Sandro I'm fine

Leonardo I killed and ate a rat with my bare hands

Sandro I'm sorry

Leonardo You already fucking said that

Beat.

When I came to this city I sought you out
I fell madly in love with you
I wanted to be with you
I wanted to *be* you

Sandro Let me kiss you

Leonardo I have the plague

Sandro I don't care

*Leonardo looks around the studio and notices the
'Birth of Venus' canvas.*

Leonardo How in God's name is that still here?

Sandro I disguised it

Leonardo How?

Sandro Threw a bunch of paint on it

Leonardo Are you going to finish it?

Sandro I renounced painting

Leonardo Oh don't give me that
The day the people have had enough
and they throw Savonarola on that fire
you're going to get right back at it
painting your nymphs and satyrs
So you lost a few years' work
A few beautiful pictures

Sandro A few beautiful pictures

Silence.

Leonardo Do you even know how it ends for Venus?
The goddess of love?
Vulcan finds her and Mars in bed
and throws a scalding iron net overtop of them
trapping them for eternity as all the gods of Olympus
    gather round and laugh at them

Silence.

You've run out of words?
Jokes?
Your old shit isn't working any more?

Sandro I . . . am a horrible person

Silence.

I –

*Leonardo turns to leave. Light shift. Spot on Sandro,
as he turns to the audience. Leonardo freezes.*

Sandro For the historians in the audience
This is the moment where, without saying a word
Leonardo turned and walked out of my life forever

Beat.

But you know what, this is my damn play
and the historians, I'm sorry, y'all can go fuck
    yourselves
Tonight we finish this
The way it should have been
With all of you as my witness

Light shift.

Sandro (*turning back to Leonardo*) Wait
Just –
I love you
I love you
Do you hear me?

Leonardo looks back.

I love you
Profoundly
More than I thought humanly possible
Every shade and hue by your hand
I can't look at a colour without seeing your hand in it
Your eyes, your lips
I love you
And and maybe I can't express it but I'm trying
I want to spend every fucking day with you
Even if it is in some godforsaken stable in Vinci

You need to eat something

Leonardo I'm not hungry

*Sandro removes a floorboard and pulls out a jar of
peanut butter, a knife, and a loaf of plain white bread.*

Sandro makes a peanut-butter sandwich and cuts it in two. Leonardo walks over and sits down beside him. Sandro hands one half of the sandwich to Leonardo.
They eat.

Sandro Was it worth it?

Leonardo Was what worth it?

Sandro All these hell fires for a bit of buggery?

Leonardo I'm not afraid
I have seen the void
And I am not afraid

Leonardo pulls the knife out of the jar of peanut butter and licks it slowly. Sandro then puts his hand over Leonardo's and licks the knife. They look at each other, holding the knife between them.
Blackout.

End of play.

.